CAPTURE
THE
MOMENT

76 Tips for Presenting to
Large Groups, Small Groups,
and One-on-One!

BY
CHUC BARNES, CSP

Warrington Press
Overland Park, Kansas

Capture The Moment
Copyright ©2005 by Chuc Barnes

ISBN: 0-9724729-1-6

Library of Congress Control Number: 2005920710

Editorial assistance by F. Barry Barnes, Professor of Management
Cover design, artwork, and page layouts by Scott Barnes

Sixth Printing: December 2009
Fifth Printing: March 2008
Fourth Printing: May 2007
Third Printing: September 2006
Second Printing: September 2005
First Printing: February 2005
Printed in the United States of America

For information contact:
Warrington Press
Overland Park, Kansas

CONTENTS

Other books by Chuc Barnes:

Get Your Ducks in A Row
(How to Better Manage Your #1 Priority — Yourself!)

Dedicated to Scott and Barry
You amaze me with your skills.

10 presenters who inspire me:
Sophie, Abigail, Teddi, Anna,
Stephen, Caroline, Matthew,
Tyler, Patrick

Ongoing appreciation to:
Brett, Todd, and Jennifer

Special thanks to my dad:
You're the first person I ever saw prepare.

INTRODUCTION

In order to share one's ideas, influence others, or achieve common goals, it's essential for successful executives to make effective presentations to groups or one on one. What happens, however, is that many plans, budgets, and sales proposals get rejected, not because the ideas in them are off target, but because the presenter or presentation is ineffective.

I contend that success is getting what you want, and that people who know how to present their ideas seem to attract success. In fact, I'll bet you can think of someone whose success accelerated because of his or her ability to present his or her ideas logically, orderly, and with a relevant, meaningful story.

The purpose of this book, therefore, is to provide you with a set of tips and guidelines to help you present your ideas with impact and to "Capture the Moment" when presenting.

The book consists of 76 tips and two worksheets, one for analyzing your audience and one for planning your presentation. The worksheets help you trigger ideas and the tips provide detailed guidance. By using the 76 tips along with the two worksheets, you'll create and deliver presentations that will tell the story you want and achieve the outcomes you're looking for.

The tips are arranged in order from what to do *first* to what to do *last* when constructing and delivering presentations. So, take a look at the two worksheets in the Appendix, and then read Tip #1 and continue reading, tip by tip, to Tip #76.

I urge you to consider these tips and worksheets for your next presentation. They'll help you gain more influence as a presenter and provide more impact for your message, no matter whether you present to a large group, small group, or one on one.

— Chuc Barnes
Certified Speaking Professional

76 Tips for Presenting to Large Groups, Small Groups and One-on-One

1. Use the Listener Analysis Worksheet and the Presentation Planning Sheet in the Appendix.

Whether you're planning to present to a large group, small group, or single individual, the worksheets in the appendix are designed to help you focus your thoughts and put many of the organizational tips described in this book into practice.

Let's suppose, for example, that you're planning to make a sales call on a group you've never met. Suppose also that you want to ask your boss for a raise. Before you begin either presentation (there's a different audience for each one), it's important to consider how both audiences think and make decisions. Use the Listener Analysis Worksheet in the Appendix to spark thoughts about your sales call audience. Use it again to remind yourself to think like your boss does when you meet with him or her.

Once you've made notes about your audience, use the Presentation Planning Sheet to construct your specific presentation for the sales call. Use it again to create your presentation for meeting with your boss.

Note: The Listener Analysis Worksheet and Presentation Planning Sheets are available in 8 x 11-inch size for free at *www.MinutesCount.com*.

2. Recognize that a good presentation tells a story and a good presenter is a good storyteller.

Everyone enjoys a story. That's what people look for in books, television shows, movies, and even on newscasts. In fact, it's what people *always* look for!

Stories make a powerful impression on the mind. They are part of our human heritage ... our oral tradition. For centuries, thoughts and ideas have been passed along through the use of stories to people who couldn't even read. In addition, good stories are repeatable so, when your presentation tells a good story, there's a chance your listener(s) will repeat it to others for you.

When creating your presentation, make certain it has all the ingredients of a good story — a beginning, middle, conclusion, and sense of drama. Too many presentations leave out one or all of these ingredients and, as a result, those presentations fall on deaf ears.

See tips 17, 18, 19, and 20 for information about using stories to dramatize *the key points in* your presentation.

3. Write out your purpose. Make sure it's clear.

An easy way to determine your purpose is to write the answer to, "Why am I delivering this presentation; what's my purpose?" To be sure you are clear, write the answer in one sentence.

See Step #2 of the Presentation Planning Sheet in the Appendix and you'll find a blank space to write down the purpose for your presentation.

4. Determine the "approach" you want to take by writing an answer to the question, "How can I make this presentation better than someone else would?"

Recognize that, as a presenter, your job is to make your content interesting, engaging, and more fascinating than it would be in a book, financial report, or chart.

In respect for your listeners' time, you want your points and content to be fresh, distinctive, and unique. The answer you give to this "how" question gives you the rationale you want.

An example would be, "I plan to illustrate each of my points with brief stories and/or examples that help my listeners see how they can apply the points I describe in their own situations."

5. Decide exactly what you want your listener(s) to do when you end your presentation.

It's important for you to know the specific action you want them to take so you can focus your presentation accordingly.

Do you want them to:

Buy
Know
Believe
Be Convinced
Change Their Mind
Understand
Approve
Recommend

See Step #3 of the Presentation Planning Sheet in the Appendix and you'll find a place to write the specific action you want your listener(s) to take when you end your presentation.

6. Put yourself in the shoes of your audience.

An audience can be one person or a group, and the more you know about how your audience thinks and makes decisions, the easier it is for you to prepare remarks that fit their thinking processes.

Note Tip #1 and you'll see examples for two different types of audiences.

Use the Listener Analysis Worksheet in the Appendix to generate thoughts about your specific audience, and record the name of your audience in Step #1 of the Presentation Planning Sheet.

7. Analyze your listener(s) in detail so you know their needs, wants, and concerns.

People listen because they want information they can use. Your listeners' time is too precious for you to talk about matters that don't interest them or help them learn.

What are their values, needs, challenges? An example might be, "I'm planning to present to a woman who values her expertise as a leader, but who needs more poise in front of an audience, and is concerned about possibly looking foolish when answering questions."

See the Listener Analysis Worksheet in the Appendix.

8. Determine the personality style(s) of your listener(s) to speed up "connection" time and bond with them.

Most of us tend to prepare for people who are exactly like us. But, unless you know your group is made up of only one or two personality styles, you'll have more success if you adjust your presentation style to reach each of the four types of listeners.

Experts have labeled the four different personality styles several different things. For simplicity, let's call them Directors, Influencers, Supporters, and Contemplators. Note the varying characteristics of each style so you'll know how to present to them in a way that best matches how they understand.

Directors:— think in terms of outcomes and bottom line. They make quick decisions and want new ideas and new methods. During presentations, they want you to get to the point, keep things moving, and stay on message.

Influencers: — are "people people" and like to talk. They are "big picture" oriented and they become bored with too many details. They love it when you pay attention to them and give them a chance to speak and interact with you or others.

Supporters:— like to see how others react to what you say. They want practical information and become uncomfortable if you call on them. They want time to think and usually don't ask questions. If they do question you, acknowledge them with appreciation.

Contemplators:— love details and want logic, accuracy, and time to think. They generally are very skeptical. They appreciate detailed handouts and thorough, well thought out answers. Be certain what you say to them is correct and don't hurry them.

If you present to *Directors*, begin on time, deal in specifics, and be brief, practical, and results-oriented.

If you present to *Influencers*, greet them when they arrive, acknowledge them, and be open and sociable. Look at them when you speak, solicit questions, and give them a chance to talk. They love having a chance to talk with the people around them.

If you present to *Supporters*, be patient and approach change slowly. Recognize that they are excellent listeners and don't expect a lot of questions from them.

If you present to *Contemplators*, take your time and be as prepared as you can be. Emphasize relevant details.

Now, suppose you don't know the styles of the people who will listen to you. First, visualize a Supporter as being the opposite of a Director, and visualize a Contemplator as being the opposite of an Influencer. If you don't know the style of your listeners, prepare for and adjust your presentation style *for your opposite style* and you'll be more apt to include ideas you might otherwise overlook.

9. Determine how much time you need to deliver your message.

An easy way to do this is to refer to the empty "Time needed" blanks on the Presentation Planning Sheet in the Appendix. Estimate the time needed for each segment (Step #5, #6, #7, #8, #9). Total the time needed for all segments and add time for questions and answers (Step #4). Add a fudge factor of several minutes so you won't feel like you have to race through your material.

Every presentation should end on time, and there's nothing better than a presentation that ends a little early. If you need more time to deliver your presentation comfortably, request it before you present, and then structure your remarks so you end a few minutes early

10. Write your conclusion before you write your introduction.

When you know the ending to your presentation, it's easier to dream up an attention-getting introduction and think of relevant points and/or story ideas.

A sample ending might be: "As you can see, the steps I've outlined make our budget planning process simpler and easier than it has been in the past."

See Step #5 of the Presentation Planning Sheet in the Appendix.

11. After you have a conclusion, write an "introduction" that attracts attention, tells listeners why it's important to them, and "sets up" your closing.

Remember the power of first impressions so give serious thought to your introduction. You want to grab the full attention of your listeners.

An example might be, "The purpose of my remarks is to discuss the budget planning process so it's easier for all of us to do."

See Steps #6 and #7 of the Presentation Planning Sheet in the Appendix.

12. Recognize how important your "opening" is.

Only a few years ago professional speakers said you only have 90 seconds to make a positive connection with an audience. The advent of MTV, cell phones, the Internet, PDAs, and laptop computers have reduced your audience's attention span considerably. Listeners size things up more quickly today.

Consider this: You now have 30 seconds to make a positive "connection" with your group. This means you need a very good opening, not just with your words, but with the way you look, the way you stand, the way you sound, and the way you conduct yourself.

13. Brainstorm ideas that you want to include after you've written your conclusion and introduction.

An easy way to do this is to use "Post-it Notes" or 3 x 5 cards. Write one idea on each card. Let the ideas flow and generate as many ideas as possible.

Eliminate your weaker ideas and try to end up with from two to five main ideas. If you have more than five ideas, reduce them by making some of them sub points.

14. Determine your sub points.

Develop sub point ideas for each main point by using "Post-It Notes" or 3 x 5 cards. Sub points may consist of explanations, data, or other evidence to support each main idea.

Arrange the sub points in order of importance for each main point from most important to least important.

It's important to rank your sub points, so you can lengthen or shorten your presentation, depending on the amount of time you have. If you need to lengthen your presentation, for example, *include* the less important points. If you need to shorten your presentation, *eliminate* the less important points.

15. Use the "power of threes" for arranging your main points so listener(s) can grasp them quickly.

Professional speakers and sales people have found that most listeners can keep track of what they say more easily when they focus on no more than three main points. When they add more points, they find that listeners tend to get confused or distracted.

Keep your objective and audience in mind and try different arrangements to see what three point arrangement works best for your message.

Examples would be:

Past, Present, Future
A, B, C
Where We Are, Where We Were, Where We're Going

If you need more than three points, add them sparingly and recognize that the more you add, the more your listener is apt to become confused.

See Step #8 of the Presentation Planning Sheet in the Appendix.

16. Consider a "10-80-10" as your organizing method.

This is sometimes described as,

> "Tell 'em what you're going to tell 'em,
> Tell 'em
> Tell 'em what you told 'em,"

"10-80-10" means 10% Introduction (Tell 'em what you're going to tell 'em), 80% Body (Tell 'em), and 10% Conclusion (Tell 'em what you told 'em). The Introduction (10%) generally consists of a "Grabber" *or* a statement of purpose or objective. The Body (80%) usually has a minimum of three points, with support for each one. The Conclusion (10%) recaps the points made and restates the grabber or purpose from the Introduction.

Using the Presentation Planning Sheet in the Appendix, as an example, a "10-80-10" would consist of:

> Step #6 - Purpose or Objective as Introduction
> Step #8 - Body
> Step #5 - Conclusion

This book follows the 10-80-10 format with an Introduction, the Body (the part you're reading now), and a Conclusion.

17. Dramatize your key points with stories or anecdotes.

Think about the way a child listens with open eyes when you tell a story. The child becomes emotionally involved and pays close attention because he or she wants to know what's going to happen next. You want the same thing to happen to your listeners.

As discussed in Tip #2, you want your entire presentation to unfold like a story. You also want to create interest and a sense of emotional involvement for your key points. To do this, incorporate stories that illustrate the points you make. Stories create "movies in the mind" and connect logically and emotionally. Stories also make you — and the points you describe — unique.

It's a good idea to jot down stories when you see them on the job or in your personal life. Maybe you see something funny happen at the airport, for example. Write it down.

Now think of a presentation you have made to someone sometime in your life. Maybe it was something you told your family. What happened, good or bad? You now have another story. Write it down. Who knows? That story might help you illustrate a point in your next presentation. Then keep watching for stories you can use in your presentations.

Professional speakers know that stories are difficult to

remember when they are under pressure to create a new presentation, so they keep notebooks of stories. Whenever they see something funny or clever, they write the details in their notebook. Then, when they prepare a new presentation, they check their notebook for a story that helps them convey the point they want to make.

It's a lot easier to come up with a "perfect" story for your presentation when you can choose from several in your notebook, rather than have to think of a story from scratch when you're hurrying to create a presentation.

18. Be certain the stories you use have messages or points that link to the ideas you talk about in your presentation.

Telling a story simply for the sake of telling a story detracts from your presentation. Be sure the stories you tell illustrate the points you deliver in your presentation.

For example, if you want to make the point that planning is important, you tell the story of Jack and Jill going up the hill to fetch a pail of water. Following the story, you might say, "Jack and Jill came tumbling down because they were unprepared. We want to prevent that from happening to us by preparing carefully for this project."

19. Contact group members prior to speaking to determine their specific needs, and listen for stories and examples from them that you might be able to use in your presentation.

Almost all professional speakers check with audience members in advance of their presentations to learn about their listeners' specific situations. Sales people do the same thing.

When you check with group members to learn what they want you to discuss, they often tell you a story or an example of a success or problem they have. Pay careful attention to what they say because their stories can be good ones for you to use to dramatize the points you make when presenting to them.

20. Try out your stories, examples, and humor with others before you use them.

Practice builds your confidence and helps you know in advance what's apt to work. Professional speakers and humorists never use stories or jokes without testing them with objective individuals first.

21. If you don't have a story, add an example or a "for instance" to each key idea to help your listeners visualize your ideas.

Examples help people envision what you describe. There are many examples in this book. *For instance*, note Tip #18.

22. Add relevant humor to lighten your message and/or to keep from taking yourself too seriously. Humor relaxes people and helps create a bond between you and your group.

When asked if humor should be included in a presentation, professional speakers jokingly say, "Only if you want to get paid." They know humor is that important to an audience.

If you don't find a funny story you can use in your "Story notebook" (Tip #17), look in a joke book. The best humor, however, comes from describing something funny that you did or noticed about yourself in the past, such as a personal flaw or mistake you made. *Note*: Humor can be *dangerous* if you direct it towards someone or some group. The *safest* humor comes when making fun of yourself.

If you use humor, keep it brief. Unless your purpose is to entertain, the best humor in a presentation is brief humor.

23. Realize that vulnerability is an asset for a confident presenter.

A professional speaker at a large meeting for professional speakers mispronounced a phrase. He attempted to correct himself and mispronounced it again. He repeated the phrase a third time and mispronounced it again. He finally looked at his audience and said, "I *are* a professional speaker" and laughed at himself. The audience immediately began laughing with him. After his presentation, person after person went to the speaker to tell him how impressed they were the way he handled his obvious error. Even though they were professionals, they knew that they too could make a mistake.

Everyone makes mistakes so be ready to laugh at yourself, if need be.

24. Make fun of yourself if something unusual goes wrong.

Too many inexperienced presenters think they need to be perfect. It's more important to be human.

If you experience misfortune by dropping something, tripping, falling, or mispronouncing a word, be ready to poke fun at yourself. Here are several expressions to use to make fun of yourself. Notice that these are expressions to help you laugh at yourself and keep going on with your presentation. They are not excuses (Tip #56) for not performing.

"I also do magic tricks."
"It took years of finishing school to learn to do that."
"I had a good trip. See you next fall."
"Tah dah!" (Put you hands in the air as if you planned it.)

When you correct what happens and proceed with your presentation, your audience tends to empathize with you and admire your ability to move forward with your message instead of being frustrated or sidetracked by the unfortunate bad luck.

25. Consider adding a metaphor, simile, alliteration, allegory, or rhyme to help your listeners " connect" with your message and retain what you say,

A **Metaphor** is a word or phrase that denotes an object or idea, but is used in place of another object or idea. Examples would be: "All the World's a stage," or "A boat without oars trying to get to shore."

A **Simile** compares two unlike things and often is introduced by the words *like* or *as*. An example would be: "The piles of paper looked like jagged mountains that no one could ever climb."

Alliteration is the repetition of initial-consonant sounds in two or more neighboring words or syllables. An example would be: "Reading, Writing, 'Rithmetic."

An **Allegory** is a story, fictional or otherwise, used to portray a truth or express a point. An example would be: "The smallest duckling said he'd rather swim on his own, but the mother duck told all the ducklings that they'd save energy and go much farther if they'd swim in a row."

A **Rhyme** can be very effective if it helps solidify a point, For example, "If the glove doesn't fit, you must acquit."

26. Anticipate any questions you think you might receive.

Write them down as you prepare so you can study them objectively. Ninety percent of the questions you'll be asked can be anticipated.

After you've written the questions, write answers to the questions. Check your answers with someone else to make sure your answers are brief, clear, and accurate.

When you prepare answers for the questions you expect, you become more relaxed.

27. Make your presentation shorter than your group expects, and always leave room for timing adjustments.

If you need *less* time (if people need to leave early for an unforeseen emergency, for instance), consider eliminating a story or suggestion.

If you need *more* time (because the person in charge asks you to speak longer, for example), add a story.

To keep track of time unobtrusively, most professional speakers place their wristwatch or a small clock on the podium where they can see it without distracting the audience from their message. Others shift their wristwatch to the underside of their wrist where they can inconspicuously see the time when speaking.

28. Consider the power of good visual aids.

Visual aids help you be as much as 43% more persuasive, and good visuals help you reduce your presentation time by as much as 40%.

Suppose you want to talk with someone about a complex problem with a computer. Realize how much time you'll save if you show them the problem on the computer itself, as opposed to describing the problem in words. That's how visual aids help you save time.

Suppose that you want to show how to prevent that complex computer problem in a presentation. You'll be more persuasive if you show how to solve the problem using the computer or a visual aid. Verbal descriptions of complex issues often confuse people, whereas visual aids help you persuade them.

Note The Presentation Planning Sheet in the Appendix. It is a visual aid that helps you visualize the steps for creating a presentation much more quickly and persuasively than the time it takes to read the points in this book.

A word of caution: If you use visuals, use them *sparingly*. One of the biggest problems in many technical presentations is the overuse of visual aids. A useful rule of thumb is one visual aid for every two minutes of presentation time.

Visual aids are powerful and are helpful for illustrating points that are hard to visualize. They should *not* be used to present simple ideas that are easily stated verbally.

29. If you use visual aids, remember that *they are not* the presenter — *you* are!

Too many people today are mistakenly counting on PowerPoint to be their presentation. You are the presenter and, if you use PowerPoint, use it only to help illustrate and anchor key ideas.

You can teach a monkey to press buttons, but monkeys can't explain "why." As a presenter, you want to explain "why."

30. Keep your visual aids simple.

The purpose of using visual aids is to help your listeners grasp and understand your message. Intricate details on visual aids tend to complicate and confuse listeners.

Simplicity helps.

Consider this: When Ernest Hemingway first began experiencing success, people say that many critics told him writing must be complex. One person challenged Hemingway to write a short story without making it complex. Hemingway proved that simplicity works by writing the following story in only six words: "For sale, baby shoes, never used."

Jerry Seinfeld says he will spend an hour editing an eight-word sentence into five words.

31. Use no more than six points on each visual.

We've all seen slides filled with text. When we see those slides, we pay attention to reading the text, rather than listening to the presenter. That often leads to misunderstandings.

To avoid "data dump" on visual aids successful presenters refer to what they call a "Rule of 6's," which means a maximum of six points per visual with a maximum of six words for each point. There are two reasons for this: 1) When you add more points on a visual aid, listeners tend to get confused and uncertain as to which point you are discussing, and 2) You have a better chance of keeping your listeners focused on you and your visual aid. Faster readers, for example, become anxious to move on whereas slower readers need more time.

It has been determined that when you use more than six words per point, your listener needs more time to grasp your meaning.

Examples would be:

> Six words are easier to grasp. (6 words)
> More than six words takes extra time. (7 words)

32. Use a large type font for your visuals (24 to 30-pt.)

It's easier for your audience to read your visuals if you use a serif typeface for bullet points and body copy. Examples are:

Times
Courier
Palatino
New York

Use a sans serif typeface for headlines. Examples are:

Helvetica
Geneva
Arial

Stay away from spelling entire words with capital letters. Words written entirely in capital letters are too difficult to read and, if you write more than seven words in capital letters, most readers will have to read those words several times to grasp the meaning you want them to receive from those words.

THIS IS NOT AS EASY TO READ. This is easier to read.

Note: Sometimes words spelled with capital letters are necessary (i.e., a company name, etc.). Treat them accordingly.

33. If you use PowerPoint, make certain that you use simple transitions and uncomplicated visual effects.

Your message is what's important to your audience — not confusing "transitions" and visual effects.

Too many inexperienced presenters today try to "dazzle" their audiences by having their words on visuals fly in from the left, the right, the top, and the bottom. This simply wears an audience out.

Make it easy for listeners to pay attention by using simple transitions like "Dissolve" and "Fade through black" and uncomplicated effects like "Blinds vertical" and "Blinds horizontal."

34. PowerPoint visuals are easier to read when you use dark backgrounds behind your copy and illustrations. Overhead transparencies work best with light backgrounds.

These are the suggestions that Microsoft, the creator of PowerPoint, makes. If you determine there will be dim lighting in the room where you present, however, you'll be better off using light backgrounds for PowerPoint.

If you're not sure what kind of lighting you'll have in the meeting room, and you use dark backgrounds, consider writing your key words in dark type and putting a box around the key words which you fill with a light color that contrasts with the dark color of the words. Note the light color boxes filled with dark type on the Presentation Planning Sheet in the Appendix.

35. Stand to the left of your visual aids unless you have a specific need to be elsewhere.

People read from left to right. Thus, when you stand to the left of your visual, your listeners will be able to look at you and read points on your visual more easily. If you stand to the right of your visual aid, it's difficult for the listener to read the visual aid and look at you at the same time.

Look at the above paragraph and pretend that someone is standing to your left and reading the paragraph to you. Now pretend that someone is standing to your right and reading the same paragraph to you. Note how difficult it is to read the paragraph and concentrate on the person to your right.

36. "Clear" your visuals when you speak so you keep the listeners' focus on you and what you say.

"Clearing," means turning to a clear page on a flip chart, turning off the light on an overhead projector, or switching to black in a PowerPoint presentation whenever you move on to a new point where the visual you've shown isn't necessary any longer.

When you "clear" visuals, you're able to see if your listeners have absorbed the material you've covered before you move forward. If they need to look at the visual longer, they'll say so without you having to ask them.

Recognize that, if you don't "clear" a visual when you move on, your group can still see the visual in front of them. Thus, there's a chance that later in your presentation a listener is apt to ask you a question about the visual, distracting you from whatever point you are discussing at that time.

37. If you use PowerPoint, press the "B" key on your laptop whenever you want the projector screen to go black to "clear" a visual, or press the "W" key if you'd prefer for the projector screen to go white.

These keys help you "clear" your visual aid, so you can respond to questions or interact with your audience without distracting the audience by having an unrelated visual aid on the screen.

38. Use the "Four T's" when moving through visuals to help keep your listeners involved.

Successful presenters know how helpful it is to:

Tease — the group to make them want to see the visual they are about to show.
Touch - the revealed visual to let the listener know which point is being discussed.
Turn - to the group and catch someone's eyes.
Tell - move forward and explain the point on the visual.

Pretend, for example, that a presenter tells you he or she is going to show you a chart that will help you save time when you make presentations. Notice how you've just been **teased** to see the visual aid.

Suppose the presenter now shows you the chart on Appendix B and **touches** the line that says, "Step #1." You now know which point they are discussing. (Note: You can touch a visual with your finger, a pointer, or by gesturing to the point on the chart you're discussing.)

When the presenter next **turns** to look at you or someone in your group, you know he or she is speaking to you and not to the visual aid.

Finally, a good presenter **tells** you why the point on the visual is important in his or her own words and not by reading the words on the visual.

39. Always have a backup plan when using visuals.

Anything can go wrong with technology, so, if you're planning to use PowerPoint, be sure to have a backup set of overhead transparencies, a prepared flip chart, or handout ready in case the computer or projector doesn't work.

40. Include any detailed information in a handout.

When you've determined how your listeners learn (See Tip #7 and #8) and how much time you have to present (See Tip #9), you'll know whether or not to have a handout at all. People who are Supporters and Contemplators, for example, want to be able to see written documentation of the points you discuss. That's the way they learn. Influencers appreciate having documentation, yet more than likely will never refer to the documentation after you present unless they want to show it to someone else. Directors want to see key points.

There will be times when you'll only have time to briefly discuss your major points in your presentation. If that's the case, you'll definitely want to give your listeners a handout so they'll have complete details.

A good handout is simply that — a handout. It does not replace you and your presentation. Pretend, for example, that this book has been given to you as a handout. As good as this book's explanations are, it still doesn't help you see how all the skills work as quickly as if a presenter showed you.

41. If you use a handout, determine when you'll distribute it so that it fits your presentation best — in advance, during, or following.

Distribute it in *advance* when you don't mind if listeners see your points before you discuss them. Distribute it *during* your presentation when you want your listeners to have additional details as you discuss the points. Distribute it *after* when you prefer to discuss your points first.

Note: If you want the handouts distributed *during* your presentation, ask listeners to hand them out for you when you want them distributed. That enables you to stay in front of the group and maintain eye contact.

Remember that handing out in advance or during your presentation causes distractions.

42. Dress like your listener(s) — formal, business casual, casual.

People tend to dress like the people that they enjoy being around. You want to dress like your listeners and to convey your respect for them add an extra touch to your attire. If your group dresses informally, for example, dress in "business casual" attire. If they dress in business casual, dress formally or at least wear a jacket. If they dress formally, dress the same and add a handkerchief (men) or scarf (women).

One thing's for sure. If your group is dressed formally and you are dressed informally, you'll look out of place and you'll miss out on the rapport that comes from common dress.

43. Relax yourself by using "relaxation" exercises before you present.

It's natural to feel a sense of "nervousness" ahead of a presentation. This is true for musicians, actors, and athletes, as well as for presenters. To help relax,

> Breathe to a slow count
> Stretch like a cat does
> Roll your head slowly so you relax your neck
> Visualize your success (Example: What will the listeners do and say? How will you feel and what will you hear from listeners when you have concluded your remarks?)

Many speakers find it helpful to put themselves in a sense of gratitude for the opportunity they have to be able to speak in front of people who want to hear what their ideas are.

44. Keep yourself from worrying ahead of your presentation by being prepared.

Preparation is the key to your success. Be sure you've filled out the Audience Analysis Sheet and the Presentation Planning Sheets in the Appendix. Be sure you've also anticipated questions (See Tip #26) and practiced your stories (See Tips 17, 18, 19, and 20) and put together your visual aids (See Tips #28 thru #39).

45. To help you be more composed and relaxed, go to the meeting room early.

One reason people get nervous when they present is that they arrive at the presentation site late and aren't acquainted with the atmosphere and the surroundings. Successful speakers go to the meeting room early. They sit in the chairs, walk on the platform, and do what they can to "own" the room. They greet listeners when they arrive so as to build a bond of trust and rapport.

46. Take charge of the area where you'll speak.

As the presenter, you are responsible for what happens between you and your listener(s).

If the microphone you need isn't right, be sure to get it fixed before you begin. Without a good microphone, your listeners will have to struggle to hear your presentation and that struggle detracts from your message. The same goes for good lighting, good seating arrangement, good prop placement, etc. See that those things are correct before you begin speaking.

47. Warm up your voice if you're going to speak for a long time.

Athletes warm up before they compete. Musicians warm up with their musical instruments before they perform in front of a group. When you speak in front of others, your voice is *your* instrument. Professional speakers warm up their voices by singing a favorite song before they present, particularly one that has notes that go up and down the scale. They also yawn several times to relax their throats before speaking.

48. Keep your mouth moist.

Avoid foods and beverages such as coffee, milk, ice, and chocolate, which dry your mouth.

Also, bring a glass or bottle of water with you. No group objects when you take a drink of water.

49. Greet people in the meeting room. Shake hands with them.

You're presenting from the moment you arrive.

As the presenter, you are a leader, and leaders set the tone. Even when you're not speaking, listeners watch you and make decisions about you as to how organized you are, how confident you are, how you treat people, and whether you "walk your talk."

50. Recognize that every audience wants you to be trustworthy, caring and compassionate about their needs, yet humble as a person and capable in your delivery.

By showing up on time, greeting people, being prepared, and speaking about the things your listeners want to hear, you have an advantage over the many people who waste the time of listeners. Some show up late, sort through notes, and talk about things that don't matter to their listeners. These same people often are unfriendly and self absorbed. In essence, they defeat rapport and wonder why their listeners don't pay attention or respond to the points they discuss.

51. Give the person who introduces you a written "introduction" of the words you want used so you'll know what is going to be said about you and aren't thrown off track when you start out.

Too often an introducer unknowingly says something about the speaker that isn't accurate or even detracts from the speaker's message. An example of a typical poor introduction is:

> *"I talked with our speaker last week and she was really funny. Here she is now and I hope she is funny again."*

Needless to say, if you're the speaker, it's difficult to be funny when you are ordered to be funny. None of this relaxes anyone.

A good introduction follows a TIC format:

T   Topic or title
I - Importance (benefits or value) of the topic to the group
C - Credentials that qualify the speaker to discuss the topic

When the TIC format is followed, the introduction helps get the listeners prepared to be involved.

An example would be:

T - *It's essential for successful people to know how to present their ideas.*

I - *You've heard about plans, budgets, or proposals that were approved or not approved because of presentation quality or weakness.*

C - *Our speaker has worked with thousands of executives who want to present themselves with impact and make the most of their time in front of an audience. His clients include (name the clients).*

Please help me welcome (presenter's name).

52. Eliminate any worry about forgetting something you want to say in your presentation by briefly listing your major points on a note card.

Simply look at your written notes, if you need them — and/or the points on your visuals — as prompts for what you want to remember to say.

Beginning presenters often attempt to memorize their entire presentation and don't realize that a totally memorized presentation sounds false and insincere.

Four things to consider memorizing, however, are:

Your introduction — so you captivate your listeners with the right phrases and tone

The points you want to make — so you remember to talk about each one

A story you plan to tell (not word for word, but certainly the key points necessary) — so you make your story as brief and to the point as possible

Your closing — so you conclude with the precise words, volume, and inflection you believe your last line needs for maximum impact

53. Be yourself and only yourself.

Too many presenters today attempt to portray themselves as something they are not, and listeners see right through them. Listeners want authenticity. They also want to know your point of view.

When you present, you're the expert.

54. Use your own material. Otherwise, you may feel less prepared.

Many people today borrow the notes and visual aids that someone else prepared and then they wonder why they are uncomfortable presenting to a group or individual.

If you know your subject and if you've prepared the words on your visual aids yourself, you'll be much more comfortable speaking in front of your listener(s).

55. If you aren't speaking from personal experience, speak as a reporter of information you've discovered.

An example of personal experience would be, "When we finally got to the bottom of the Grand Canyon, Phantom Ranch looked rustic and refreshing to me."

An example of reporting information you've discovered would be, "The book explained that Phantom Ranch looks rustic and refreshing to hikers when they get to the bottom of the Grand Canyon."

56. Never ask for sympathy or make excuses for normal fears.

Beginners and poorly prepared presenters often try to gain sympathy from their listeners by telling their audience, "I'm nervous" or "I've lost my thought and can't think." They overlook the fact that presenting takes courage and that courageous people don't complain. Courageous people do what they can to move forward.

Make the most of your time in front of your listeners by professionally moving on in your presentation, no matter what happens. If you are nervous, never tell your listener, "I'm nervous" as an excuse for not performing because that will make them nervous too. If you lose your thought, check your notes or your visuals, instead of saying, "I've lost my thought," which simply makes your listener feel as if you are unprepared and wasting their time.

See Tip #24 for suggestions about what you might say to lighten the mood when you deal with an unexpected misfortune.

57. Keep your focus on your listener(s), instead of thinking about yourself.

Recognize that when you make a presentation, you are the expert. Your listeners don't know what you're going to say, and they don't know what you are going to show them. They want you to be interesting and not waste their time. If you've planned your presentation, your stories and your visuals, and if you're respectful of their time, you'll be giving them what they want.

Nervous presenters, who worry about how they look, how their voice sounds, or some personal flaw, make themselves more nervous by focusing on themselves.

58. Work for stage "presence" when speaking, so that your listener(s) can more easily focus on you and what you say.

To avoid distractions, stand up straight and plant your feet firmly on the floor.

Move only when you want to make a transition or to emphasize a point. Make sure any walking you do is *deliberate* and that you don't wander or fidget. Wandering makes listeners feel restless or nervous, the same way an actor wants them to feel when the actor wanders or fidgets to convey nervousness in a play.

59. Recognize how much your body language affects your message.

Effective communication comes from three elements:
Non-verbal (what people see) — 55%
Tone of voice — 38%
The actual words you use — 7%

This often shocks people who see the data the first time because many are convinced that words are most important. Words are important. They are as important as you've always known them to be, but — to be an effective communicator — it's important for the Words to be congruent with the Sound and the Non-verbal, such as body language. If they aren't, the listeners pick out what they hear in the tone (Sound), or what they see in the body language (Non-verbal), and ignore the Words. Those mixed messages hinder communication.

Successful presenters make the most of the 55% Non-verbal parts of communication by avoiding these actions that detract from their message:

Hands in pockets (it's hard for listeners to trust you when your hands are hidden)
Hands held behind your back
Arms crossed or folded
Hands in a fig leaf position
Wringing hands

Fidgeting with fingers or jewelry

You'll find Tone of voice suggestions in Tips #64 and #65.

There are some Non-verbal suggestions in Tips #60, #61, #62, and #63.

60. Recognize the importance of smiles.

Smiles are contagious. Smiles relax you and your audience. People cherish appropriate smiles.

Smiles also enhance your energy.

61. Be sure to use natural gestures when you speak.

Gestures help you deliver ideas with fewer words and they assist memory.

Think, for example, about a fisherman. Does he tell you how big the fish he caught was, or does he show you how big it was with his hands? When he shows you the size, he doesn't need as many words as he would have needed if he had only *told* you about the fish's size. Not only that, you can more easily *remember* what you saw the fisherman *show* you with his hands.

Your listeners want to trust you and it's easier for them to trust you if they can see your hands. Keep your hands in front of you and outside of your pockets. If you are fidgeting with your hands, your listeners will conclude that you are nervous and unsure about what you are saying.

62. Maintain sensible eye contact with your listeners.

Beginning presenters often struggle to look at every listener in the room. This makes them and their listeners uncomfortable.

When you have more than one listener, don't scan the entire group. Instead, focus on one person for a few moments and then move to another person in a different area so you actually are having mini conversations with a variety of people in your audience.

63. Get as physically close to your listener(s) as you can without invading personal space.

Closeness builds rapport and rapport builds trust.

If you're speaking one on one, do what you can to eliminate any barrier between you and the listener and position yourself to sit or stand side by side when speaking. Remember, however, that personal space varies from culture to culture.

64. Speak in your normal voice and increase your natural volume a bit.

The increased volume conveys confidence to your listeners.

You want drama in your presentation so be certain you vary your voice level from time to time to arouse listener interest and provide surprise in what you're saying.

Never yell to be heard — you'll alienate everyone! If you think you need to yell to be heard, get a microphone *or*, if a microphone is not available, move closer to your listeners.

65. Use a microphone whenever you are speaking to 30 or more people, but be sure to use it correctly.

Microphones help you be heard more clearly.

Talk "across" a microphone, rather than speaking directly into it. And if you're using a handheld microphone, keep it a minimum of two inches away from your mouth.

66. If you are leading a traditional team meeting, use a "PAL".

A PAL is an acronym that means:

P - Purpose/People
A - Agenda/Activities/Actions
L - Limit/Leader

In other words, you don't want to have a meeting without knowing clearly what the Purpose is (this gives focus) and who the People are that you need in the meeting. This means that if the Purpose of the meeting is to make decisions and the decision makers aren't there, call off the meeting.

Next, you want Agenda items that help you fulfill your Purpose. Also, you want Activities (i.e., discussion, brain-storming, group reports, etc.) that help your team accomplish the Actions of the meeting's goal.

Lastly, add time Limits so attendees know when the meeting will end. Respect your group enough to know they have bodily functions to take care of and priority calls they need to return.

(Note: The Leader's function is to see that the points of the PAL are handled, Purpose determined, People invited, Agenda created and sent, Activities determined, Time lines set, Actions recorded.)

67. In a team meeting recognize that as a speaker, you're a leader, and effective leaders pay attention to their team.

Children will believe anything you say; yet adults generally have a skeptical mind and a head full of thoughts. Just as important, adults don't want their time wasted.

When it's time for the team meeting to begin, begin. Start by describing the Purpose (to get group focus) and move to your first Agenda subject. When the first subject has been handled, ask your group what Actions and Decisions you and the group need to make as a result of that first agenda item. Record Action and Decision items opposite the Agenda item.

Move on to Agenda item two and, when complete, record the Actions and Decisions you determine. You want recorded "Actions" and/or "Decisions" for each agenda item. This makes your meeting more inviting, productive, and focused.

Make sure your Agenda includes Assignments, where you assign all the Actions and Decisions to the various individuals on your team, spreading the work around to all. Now, your team leaves the meeting knowing who's doing what, and when. Best of all, you don't end up having to do all the work yourself.

If your meeting is a *videoconference or teleconference*, e-mail or fax a copy of the Agenda with Actions and Decisions included to each participant. Doing this, you replace old-fashioned Minutes, which you definitely don't want because they waste time and, not only that, they encourage people to say things just to get their names in the Minutes. It's the action items your group determines that count.

68. If you are participating in someone else's meeting, use a "PAL" to organize your report.

An example would be:

P - "The *Purpose* of my presentation is...."
A - "I'll be covering these three *Agenda* items..."
L - "I'll *Limit* my remarks to 7 or 8 minutes."

69. When you've begun your presentation, tell the listeners when you'd like for them to ask questions, *during or following* your presentation, depending on your time frame.

Listeners might not have questions, but they always want to know when they can ask questions if they think of them.

70. Solicit questions when you are ready for them.

Ask, "What questions do you have?" rather than saying, "Do you have any questions?" The "What" question indicates you expect questions, whereas the "Do you?" question says you are only wondering if they have questions.

If you want questions and don't get any, say, "A question I thought you'd ask is..." Then answer it and say, "What questions do you have?" so you'll prompt possible questions and let your listeners know that you do indeed want to answer any questions they have. If they don't have a question when you've asked a second time, accept the fact that there are no questions and proceed with your presentation.

71. Validate every question you receive.

Simply say, "Thank you, that's a good question," or "Good question, I didn't explain that and am happy to do so now," or "Good for you, I thought I included everything when I put my material together, but that's a point I missed."

72. Summarize before you close. (Tell 'em what you told 'em.)

If you've done your job right, you will have covered several points before you end, so recap them before you close. There are two reasons for doing this. First, you want to remind your listener of the points you've made. Second, listeners sometimes let their minds wander when you speak, and you want to be certain your listener has heard each point you've made.

73. Conclude with a crescendo — not "thank you"

Your entire presentation should be building towards your last line. To help your listeners remember your final thought, recognize that adults, unlike children, have a head full of distractions and they tend to remember the last thing they hear. Thus, if you want to thank your listeners, do so before your ending so the last words your listeners hear are the ones you say in your conclusion.

An example would be:

"Thank you for your questions and your professionalism. You've been a great group to speak with today."

"The thought I want to leave you with is that — just as FDR said — 'We have nothing to fear, but fear itself' — so use these skills in all your presentations and they'll help you have the influence and presentation impact you want."

74. Know your closing line by heart.

Your closing is the highlight of your presentation and should be a logical conclusion. You want it to be short, sweet, and with a punch. Make sure it calls for the action you want (the what, the how, and the when) and that you can deliver it in 30 seconds.

An example would be:

"I urge you to begin — starting today — to use these tips for all your presentations and you'll quickly notice more influence for yourself as a presenter and more impact on your audience for the ideas you present."

75. Enjoy yourself.

Many professional speakers write the word "fun" on a card and put it where they can see it while presenting to remind themselves to have fun and not take themselves too seriously.

76. Practice presenting by speaking anytime you can.

The best presenters realize that presenting is a skill and, thus, the more they practice, the better they get.

Look for opportunities to speak to large groups, small groups, or one on one. Perhaps you could deliver a presentation to your church, temple, Rotary Club, business meeting, or friend. Or maybe you'd like to hone your skills by attending a Toastmasters meeting. Toastmasters International is an excellent place to practice in a safe, structured environment where the members show up to practice speaking and help each other improve.

Practice makes perfect.

CONCLUSION

As I said in the Introduction, the purpose of this book is to provide you with a set of tips and guidelines to help you present your ideas with impact and to "Capture the Moment" when presenting.

Please notice, incidentally, that this book — *like a truly good presentation* — unfolds like a story, follows a logical order, and is organized around a "10-80-10" (Tell 'em what you're going to tell 'em, Tell 'em, and Tell 'em what you told 'em).

I urge you to use the tips in this book. I genuinely believe that, if you do, you'll achieve more success in your presentations and become one of those people whose success accelerates because of your improved ability to present your ideas logically, orderly, and with relevant, meaningful stories.

I know from 20 years of professional speaking and from coaching thousands of executives on their presentation skills that these tips work.

— Chuc Barnes
Certified Speaking Professional

Appendix A

LISTENER ANALYSIS WORKSHEET

1. What do I want to accomplish by presenting to this person or group?

2. Values that need to be considered for this person or group?
   (What's important to them?)

3. Constraints that must be recognized for this person or group?
   (What might hold them back from doing what I want them to do or knowing
   what I want them to know?)

4. Special needs of this person or group?

5. How do I rate the listener's topic and technical knowledge:

   High _____ Low _____ Mixed _____ Unknown _____

6. My assessment of listeners' willingness to accept the ideas I present:

   High _____ Low _____ Mixed _____ Unknown _____

7. Listener's opinion of me as a speaker prior to the presentation:

   High _____ Low _____ Mixed _____ Unknown _____

8. Examples of supporting ideas and arguments likely to work well:

9. Examples of supporting ideas likely to cause a negative reaction:

10. Stories or examples the listener has described:

11. What personality styles seem to be represented?

    Directors _____ Influencers _____ Supporters _____ Contemplators _____ Unknown _____

Appendix B

PRESENTATION PLANNING SHEET
(to help me "Capture the Moment")

Step #1: Who's the audience?_____

Step #2: What's my purpose?_____

Step #3: What do I want the audience to do?

Buy_____ Believe_____ Change mind___ Approve_____

Know___ Be convinced__ Understand___ Recommend__

Step #4: What's the time frame? Time allotted_____ Time needed (add #5, #6, #7, #8, #9)

Step #6: Purpose or objective:

Time needed? _____

> Grabber or statement of objective

Step #7: Tie to audience:

Time needed? _____

> Why important to audience

Step #8: Body:

Time needed? _____

> Point #1 with example, story, or for instance

Time needed? _____

> Point #2 with example, story, or for instance

Time needed? _____

> Point #3 with example, story, or for instance

Step #9: Recap:

Time needed? _____

> Summarize points made

Step #5: Conclusion:

Time needed? _____

> Drive closing home